THE
OTTAWA

by Barbara McCall and Kathi Howes

Illustrated by Katherine Ace

ROURKE PUBLICATIONS, INC.

VERO BEACH, FLORIDA 32964

CONTENTS

Library of Congress Cataloging-in-Publication Data

McCall, Barbara A., 1936-
  The Ottawa / by Barbara McCall and Kathi Howes.
    p.   cm. —(Native American people)
  Includes index.
  Summary: Examines the history, culture, and present-day status of the Ottawa Indians, one of the Northeast Woodland tribes of the Great Lakes.
    1. Ottawa Indians—Juvenile literature. [1. Ottawa Indians. 2. Indians of North America.] I. Howes, Kathi, 1938- II. Title. III. Series.
  E99.O9M33 1992   977'.004973—dc20   91-28111
  ISBN 0-86625-394-7   CIP
                                                                      AC

INTRODUCTION

The Ottawa people are one of the Northeast Woodland tribes of the Great Lakes. Their villages once stretched along the shores of Lake Huron and Lake Michigan. They also made their homes on the northern islands where these two lakes join, and in southeastern Canada. These places are still home to many Ottawa people today.

Before white people came to the Lakes region, the Ottawa lived peaceably with their neighbors the Chippewa—often called Ojibwe—and the Potawatomi. These three tribes still have a close relationship. The Ottawa refer to the Chippewa as the "older brothers" and the Potawatomi as the "younger brothers." They all speak the Algonquian language that is common to most of the Eastern tribes.

The forested lands of the early Ottawa were filled with hardwood trees such as birch, beech, sugar maple, basswood, elm, cedar, and oak. The tribe discovered many uses for each kind of tree. One tree, the birch, was the source of something very special—the birchbark canoe. The Ottawa were master craftsmen of this canoe, which all others envied. It allowed the Ottawa to travel easily and swiftly through the waterways around them.

The Ottawa were known to friends and enemies alike as the most skillful users of the birchbark canoe. Perhaps that skill helped them develop their talent and fame as traders. In fact, the name Ottawa comes from the word *a da we*, which means "to trade." The Ottawa bartered with other tribes. They traveled the lakes and rivers in their canoes, which they loaded with a great variety of goods: corn, sunflower oil, beaver fur pelts, animal skins, rugs, tobacco, and medicinal herbs and roots.

As French explorers and traders entered the area in the 1600s, they developed a friendly fur trading business with the Ottawa and other tribes. The relationship continued for more than a hundred years. The Ottawa, however, did not have a good relationship with the British military, which entered the region in large numbers in the 1700s.

It was during this time that Pontiac, a great Ottawa leader, made his mark in history. He united many tribes to fight the British. Under his leadership, the Native Americans pushed the British out of forts in the Ohio River Valley and along Lake Erie. It was a temporary victory.

After the American Revolution, the lives of all Native Americans changed. The citizens of the newly created United States of America gradually took over most of the lands of America's native people. These Native Americans have not vanished. Today, Michigan is home to many descendents of the early Ottawa.

Lake Superior
THE OTTAWA
MICH.
Lake Huron
WISCONSIN
Lake Michigan
MICHIGAN
L. Ontario
Lake Erie
PENNSYLVANIA
ILLINOIS
INDIANA
OHIO

CANADA

U.S.A.

MEX.

The OTTAWA

Wigwam Builders

IN the 1500s, the Ottawa made few permanent homes. The tribe was mostly nomadic—wandering from place to place in search of new hunting and fishing grounds. Whole families moved together and set up easy-to-build shelters called wigwams.

Over time, these people settled in larger communities and built homes that resembled the longhouse of their Iroquois neighbors. A longhouse was a rectangular structure, sometimes as large as 20 feet wide and 100 feet long. It could hold nine families. That style of home became the Ottawas' summer home. The wigwam, from which they did most of their hunting

and fishing, continued to be their winter home.

The wigwam was a circular, dome-shaped structure big enough for just one or two families. Women and children had the job of building the family's wigwam. It was a simple structure that they could put together in a short time. The materials were used again and again, each time the wigwam was set up in a new location. The frame was often left in place to be reused the next year.

The frame of the wigwam was made with 15 or 20 poles cut from young saplings, each about 3 inches in diameter. The women first drew a circle on the ground, about 15 feet across, to mark the shape of the dwelling. Next, they stood the poles in the ground about 2 feet apart around the circle. Each pole was then arched and tied to the opposite pole across the circle. Other poles were tied in rings around the arched frame to make the wigwam stable.

The wigwam frame was covered with cattail mats and weatherproof birchbark strips that were prepared during the summer months. The mats and strips were easily rolled and stored when not in use.

The strips were made from pieces of birch bark sewed together to form runners 2 feet wide and 6 feet long. The cattail mats were smaller, about 2 feet by 4 feet. To make these mats, the women first gathered cattails in the fall and left them to dry until spring. Then they peeled the outer layer off each stalk

and laid the flexible, stripped stalks side by side. Next, they sewed or tied the stalks together. While they worked on the mats, the women sprinkled the cattail reeds with water to keep them soft and manageable.

Inside the wigwam, sleeping platforms were placed around a central fire. The platforms were made of layers of tree branches and grasses, covered with skins and mats. A fire burned all the time, with the smoke curling up through a smoke-hole in the roof. The family, busy with hunting chores outside, did not spend much time inside the hut. It was a place to sleep and store their few possessions. But most important, the wigwam provided protection against the harsh winds and snows of the cold winter nights.

Riches of the Land

The lands of the Ottawa provided them with a rich supply of food. These Native Americans fished, hunted, and gathered wild rice and berries.

Families usually had a supply of dried corn, obtained either from trading or from farming. Ottawa farms were not at all like farms today. It was too hard to clear trees from the land, so the Ottawa often looked for open spaces with few trees. Then they planted corn, beans, and squash *between* the trees!

The Ottawa had a variety of ways to prepare food for eating. They dried squash, nuts, and berries, and pressed them into cakes. The Ottawa also were clever cooks. Many of their methods we still use today.

The favorite Ottawa way to cook was out in the open over a small fire. The Ottawa did not use big bonfires. Frequently, just three sticks made a

good cooking fire. Fresh meat was skewered on green sticks—young and freshly picked tree branches—and broiled over the little fire. Sometimes the meat was cooked in a birchbark container. Stones, heated to white-hot, were placed in the container along with the meat and some water. The hot stones cooked the food. Cooks also fried meat on flat stones, using raccoon fat as we use butter or oil today.

Another Ottawa food-preparation technique was to hang a cooking vessel at the end of a slanting pole, and position the container over the fire. The opposite end of the pole was stuck into the ground at an angle, and pinned down with a short, forked stick. The forked stick, in turn, was anchored by a good-sized stone.

The Ottawa did most of their big game hunting in the fall, winter, and spring. Deer and moose were hunted mainly in winter. The Ottawa liked small game, too. They hunted muskrat, grouse, porcupine, rabbit, wolf, squirrel, otter, marten, and mink. Each family hunted the same areas each year. They considered a hunting area their own special place and often staked it out with markers or other symbols so that others would not hunt there.

The Ottawas' hunting grounds were not close to their villages. Often, when they had a long distance to travel, families lived at the hunting grounds for a whole season, constructing wigwams. The best way to travel to and from hunting grounds was on water. Canoes were fast and made it easy to carry the heavy meat home.

The Ottawa depended on two special hunting skills: silence and careful tracking. They needed these skills because their bows didn't have a very long shooting range. The farthest bow shot was about 125 feet. By moving through the woods silently, taking care not to snap twigs underfoot or rustle underbrush, the hunters could take their prey by surprising it close up. Even Ottawa children learned early to track animals. They paid attention to the habits of game, and became expert at "reading" different animal tracks. Setting traps was another good way to hunt.

Moose was probably the most important part of the Ottawas' meat diet. Winter snow made it easiest to catch moose because the hunters, wearing large snowshoes, could move quickly over the ice and snow. The snowshoes looked something like a modern-day tennis racquet. Each shoe had an oval

frame with webbing stretched across it; a deerskin shoe was attached to each frame. Snowshoes gave the hunters a big advantage because in wearing them they could move quickly in pursuit of their slow-moving prey.

There was another trick the Ottawa hunters used with great success. They wore animal skins and antlers to fool the moose! Disguised as moose, the hunters could sneak close enough to the animals to be able to use their bows and arrows at close range.

Wild rice was a natural crop that Ottawa families used as a basic food. They didn't plant it but they did harvest it. Wild rice develops in thick clusters at the tips of a tall kind of grass. Rice plants grew in shallow, muddy water near the shores of lakes and ponds. The Ottawa poled canoes single file through the rice grass and whacked the tops of the rice plants with sticks. That loosened the grains, making them fall onto mats that had been placed in the canoes' bottoms. Later, the rice grain was dried and put into special holes in the ground lined with skins. Next, the men stomped the grains to separate the kernels from their small, hard, outer layer. Then the women sorted the rice, discarding the hard casings and saving the rice which they stored in soft baskets. To protect the rice, it was also wrapped in birch bark before it was stored underground.

Fishing

Fishing was an important source of food for the Ottawa. They lived near big lakes, streams, and ponds to maintain a fresh supply of fish.

The Ottawa had many different ways to fish. Some of them waded into the water with spears, and speared their catch. Others launched their spears from big rocks or canoes. Another way to lure the fish was to mash up poison weeds and dump them into a slow stream. When the fish died from the poison plants, children were sent into the stream to gather the fish as they floated to the top of the water. This kind of fishing produced a good catch, but it wasn't very popular with the children! The mashed-up poison pokeberries and jack-in-the-pulpit roots in the water irritated their skin.

Plenty of fish were caught with hooks and bone gorges, too. Bird wish-bones—the v-shaped parts of birds' breastbones—were often shaped into fishhooks. Bone gorges were straight pieces of bone less than an inch long. A gorge was sharp at both ends with a line tied to its middle. When a fish swallowed the baited gorge, the person fishing jerked the line and the gorge turned crossways, sticking in the throat of the fish. The fish could then be pulled from the water.

By far the most popular way to fish was with nets. The entire village helped to string large nets between two long poles driven into the lake or river bottom. One pole was close to shore. The other pole was brought farther out into the water by many braves in canoes. The net floated just beneath the surface of the water. When the net was full of fish, the people, some in canoes and others in the water, pulled the far end of the net around to meet the part of the net close to shore. That way, hundreds of fish were caught in the nets. It was quite a splashy affair! Both people and fish flopped about in the water. It was tough work to drag the heavy nets in the water.

Making Maple Sugar

The Ottawa had a sweet tooth. Their "candy" was maple sugar gathered every spring from the family sugarbush. A sugarbush is a stand of trees that are mostly maples. Each year, the family returned to its own sugarbush camp. The camp consisted of a wigwam for storing birchbark pails and other sugar-making equipment. Another larger wigwam was used to boil the sticky sap gathered from the trees.

It wasn't too hard to collect a maple tree's sweet liquid treasure. The family cut a sideways slit in the trunk about four feet from the ground. Next, they pounded a cedar spike into the slit at an angle that would help the sap drop from inside the tree into a birchbark pail that was attached to the tree.

The next step was to cook the sticky liquid in a big container with heated stones inside. The cooks used small paddles to stir the sap until they saw strings of maple syrup hanging from the stirring paddle. If the cooking was continued, the heated stones and the stirring worked even more magic—the syrup began to thicken into sugar. Then, the sugar was left to cool and harden. Later, the workers used their hands and a paddle to break the sugar into clumps that could be easily stored.

Maple sugar showed up at important feasts and ceremonies. It was also used in daily life on fruits, vegetables, cereal—even on fish! Because the Ottawa had no salt, their main seasoning was sugar. Maple sugar was considered a special treat, too. Children ate it like candy. And Ottawa mothers, like mothers today, helped their children swallow medicine more easily. They mixed maple sugar with medications to make them taste better.

Sports and Games

Like most Native Americans, the Ottawa loved competitive games, and they liked to bet on the outcomes.

Games of hiding and guessing were always favorites. One such game was called the moccasin game. In it, the Ottawa used four moccasins to cover four objects such as pebbles, small bones, or fruit pits. One of the objects was marked. Players used a three-foot rod to point to the moccasin they

believed hid the marked object. It sounds like a simple game, but the Ottawa loved playing it and got quite excited as each player took a turn at guessing and pointing.

An early form of lacrosse was another favorite game. The Ottawa used curved sticks with small nets to catch and toss a wooden ball. Their teams for this game were huge, unlike lacrosse teams today.

Snowsnake was the game played most often in winter in Ottawa villages. It required ice and snow. Players dragged a huge log through the snow to make an icy track about the length of five modern-day football fields. The snakes

were sticks made of maple wood. Each snake was about an inch and a half thick. Nearly as tall as a man, the snakes were very smooth and tapered toward the tail with a notch for the player's finger. At the other end of the stick, a head was carved to look like a real snake.

The object of the game was to throw the snake underhanded as hard as possible down the track. Once the snake hit the icy ground, it slid over the long track. The distance each snake traveled was measured. Then the spot was marked by sticking the snake upright in the snow. The thrower whose snake traveled farthest won all the snakes.

The Naming Ceremony

When an Ottawa infant was about a year old, it was the custom to give the child a formal name. This was a special event, similar to the christening ceremony some children have today. The young Ottawa mother dressed her tiny child in little deerskin moccasins decorated with porcupine quills that had been dyed bright colors. Then the baby, wearing a loincloth, was wrapped snugly in a blanket. A loincloth is a brief garment that hangs from the waist.

Along with the ceremony, a great party with wonderful food was held for all the relatives and friends. The sacred part of the ceremony was to find a name that was just right for the child.

The invited relatives and guests sat in a circle and waited for their medicine man to begin the ceremony. Medicine men were important figures in Native American life. Part holy men and part healers, they were believed to have supernatural powers.

As the ceremony began, the baby's mother and father would, in turn, announce their own names and identify their tribal background. As they gave their personal history, the tiny child was passed from relative to relative for inspection. Then the medicine man called on all the *manitos* to look upon the baby. The manitos were the good and bad spirits that the Ottawa believed held power in the spirit world. The medicine man called upon Kitchi Manitou, the Great Spirit and Master of Life. He asked Kitchi Manitou to command the good spirits to favor all Ottawa and especially the child to be named that day.

Next, a fire was started, and tobacco placed in it so that everyone could see the

smoke and smell the strong tobacco. Then Kitchi Manitou was asked to make a sign so that the people would know what to name the child. The medicine man held the baby up to face all directions while everyone waited for a sign.

It is said that Pontiac, the great Ottawa chief, was named when a brave who was running along the water's edge suddenly stopped short and then started off again. *Pon-di-ak* was the word for "stopping up the pathway." There's no way of knowing for sure whether this is how Pontiac got his name. Certainly many Ottawa boys and girls got their names from some unusual occurrence or an animal that caught the attention of the medicine man who was given the job of naming the child.

The Bear Feast

The Ottawa did not like to kill bears. They believed that the bear had helped their tribe in times past. One story tells of an Ottawa brave who was saved from an enemy tribe when he hid in a bear cave. The bear did not hurt the brave or give away his hiding place. Another legend says that the Ottawa first learned to hunt for food by following a bear.

Occasionally, it was necessary to hunt the bear. Bear oil was used for cooking and bear fur provided bedding and clothing. And certainly bear meat was delicious to eat.

When an Ottawa family killed a bear, it was an occasion for a special ceremonial feast to honor the bear. First, the family built a frame with a platform many feet above the ground. The high frame kept animals from stealing the family's prize.

At the feast, the bear's head was decorated with beads and ribbons and laid out on a mat near its fur skin. Its ears were decorated with silver arm bands, and a twist of tobacco was fastened under the bear's nose. Then, a wampum belt, an Indian ceremonial belt made of shells, was laid across its eyes. Berries, maple sugar, and other foods that bears like to eat were placed near the animal as an offering. The tribe also laid out fine clothing for the bear's spirit to wear.

During the feast, the family smoked a special pipe and took turns blowing smoke into the bear's face. The Ottawa believed that the smoke would calm the bear's anger over being killed.

(Photo courtesy of Bettmann Archive, NY)

Pontiac and his men meeting with Major Rogers and his troops.

Tobacco and the Sacred Pipe

Tobacco was very important in most Native American cultures. Native Americans believed it was a special gift from the spirit world. The Ottawa, too, used tobacco in all important ceremonies. A few pinches of dried tobacco leaf were sprinkled on the waters where rice grew to ensure a good harvest. The Ottawa also sprinkled tobacco around trees and animals that were deformed. The natives believed that the tobacco would protect them from the anger of the spirit that had caused the strange shape.

Tobacco was also used as a form of communication among tribes. Invitations to a feast were often accompanied by a pinch of tobacco. At important events, tobacco was smoked in a special pipe called a calumet. The name probably came from the French word for *flute* because this special pipe reminded French traders of a flute.

The pipestem, often as long as 17 inches, was decorated with feathers and attached to a carved stone bowl.

The calumet was called a peace pipe because smoking it with enemies often signaled the end of war. It was also smoked when the tribe's council decided to begin a war. The calumet had many peacetime uses, too. Few ceremonies were conducted without it. It was used in rituals that asked the spirits for rain. It was present, too, when the Ottawa gave thanks for good crops or a successful hunt. The peace pipe was also smoked when welcoming a stranger.

In tribes that used the calumet, there was always one particular calumet considered to be the most powerful. It was the tribe's prized possession. Because it was so valuable, one tribe member had the job of guarding this pipe. He was also chosen to become familiar with all the ceremonies that used the pipe. He then led the other tribe members through those parts of the sacred rituals that used the pipe.

Moosehides and Porcupine Quills

The northern woodlands where the Ottawa lived were very cold for half of the year. The moose that roamed the forests were the source of the people's warm outer clothing. Boots, jackets, and head coverings were made from moosehide, with all its thick, coarse hairs left in place.

The Ottawa carefully skinned different parts of the moose to make different items of clothing. The shoulder and foreleg of the animal became ready-made sleeves for garments. The skin around the joint of the moose's hind leg was the perfect shape for the heel of a boot. Larger skins were sewn together to complete the outer garments. Moose and bear skins also made warm winter blankets.

During the late spring and summer, the Ottawa, like most Native Americans of the Northeast, dressed only in soft, light deerskin clothing. In the warmest weather, the men usually wore just a breechclout. The breechclout, also known as a breechcloth, was a piece of fabric about 18 inches wide that passed between the legs. The ends of the cloth were draped over a belt at the waist and hung down to the knees in front and back. Women wore only a skirt or a sleeveless dress made of two deerskins sewn together at the shoulders and belted at the waist.

Often the women decorated the family's clothing with porcupine quills. A porcupine quill is hollow, and it can be pulled easily from the animal's fur. One animal can provide thousands of quills. The quills are white with dark tips, but the Ottawa colored them with berry juice. Quills were added to the fringe of garments. They were also formed into strips or bands by placing many quills over a piece of lightweight fiber. The bands could be shaped into designs and used to decorate moccasins and other pieces of clothing.

Quillwork was also used to decorate birchbark boxes. Finished quillwork looks similar to woven straw. By the 1800s, many white people discovered the beautiful quillwork of the Ottawa and their neighbors. Native American girls spent many hours creating quillwork items that were sold to whites.

The Birchbark Canoe

The Ottawa and the Chippewa were master builders of the graceful and swift birchbark canoe. Birch bark is a wonderful material. It is lightweight, windproof, and waterproof. It can be easily rolled and folded, and when it is heated, it can be shaped into boxes and other containers.

Building a canoe was a two- or three-week project for several families. The process began in the spring, the best time of year to strip a tree of bark that was strong and flexible.

First, the men cut down one or two white cedar trees. Cedar was strong, yet easy to bend and shape into the inside parts of the canoe: the ribs, rails, and the side planking. The cut cedar was usually stored under water to keep it pliable until the men were ready to construct the frame of the canoe. Next, the men cut several birch trees and stripped the bark lengthwise. To make one canoe, they needed three long strips. One strip was for the bottom of the boat. The other two strips would form the sides.

The women dug the roots of spruce and tamarack trees to make sewing fibers. They also collected sap and resin from pine trees to make a glue-like substance that would be used to seal the seams of the canoe.

When all materials were gathered, the building began. A flat area was selected as the work site. The men pounded two rows of posts into the ground to outline the shape and length of the canoe. One strip of bark was laid the length of the

canoe between the posts and covered with heavy rocks to keep the bark from curling. Then the men trimmed the other two strips to shape the sides and ends of the boat.

Next, the women glued the side strips to the bottom piece before beginning to sew the seams where the strips over-lapped. One woman carefully poked holes along the seam, and another woman sewed by pulling the root fibers through the holes. When the shell of the canoe was finished, the men worked on the inside of the boat. They laid thin, narrow strips of cedar side by side over the length of the birch bark. Next, the ribs—U-shaped pieces—were put in place across the canoe to give the boat its shape. Then the men lashed the top edges of the bark to cedar rails, called

gunwales, which the men had prepared earlier. Several crossbars of different lengths were added to keep the rails apart and further shape the width of the boat.

The men and women worked together to shape and sew the high, rounded front and back ends of the boat. This unique rounded design identified the Ottawa or Chippewa birchbark canoe.

While the canoe was taking shape, it was always kept moist so that the bark would not split or crack. But when all parts were finished, the boat was left to dry. Finally, the canoe was ready for sealing. The women spread all the seams with a hot mixture made from charcoal, grease, and the tree resins they had collected earlier. The boat was now completely watertight and ready for use.

Pontiac had dealings with several British
commands in his fight to keep his people free.
Here he and his braves negotiate with Major Gladwyn.

Pontiac and a white man dressed as a frontiersman engage in a pow-wow.
(Photo courtesy of Bettmann Archive, NY)

The Great Traders

The Ottawa were the great traders among both other Native American tribes and whites in the Northeast and the Great Lakes area. Trade routes along the rivers and lakes were controlled by individual Ottawa families. The leader of the family gave or denied permission to others to use the routes. Those who used the routes illegally had to pay a fine, such as food or furs. Some trespassers were killed. The Ottawa often arranged marriages between powerful families to strengthen their control over the trade routes.

By the 1600s, the French had set up trading posts along the St. Lawrence River. They exchanged their European-made goods—metal knives, needles, axes,

kettles, and guns—for fur pelts collected by the native people. In the early days of trading, the Ottawa were middlemen. They exchanged their corn for Chippewa fur; then they traded the fur to the powerful Huron who, in turn, traded directly with the French.

By 1649, the Huron were defeated by the Iroquois. This ended Huron power and Huron influence with the French. From that time through 1700, the Ottawa traded directly with the French, traveling by canoe to faraway places such as Montreal and Quebec, Canada.

The Ottawa and the French had a good relationship for many years. The Ottawa grew to depend upon the European-made goods they bartered. Traders married Ottawa women and set up their homes near native villages. When the

French military went to war with the British in North America, the Ottawa people sided with the French.

From the late 1600s through 1760, French and English forces fought to control the land between the Appalachian Mountains and the Mississippi River. The French controlled Canada as well as Louisiana. They wanted to connect the two areas by setting up a chain of forts along the rivers. The British, too, wanted to control that area.

In 1755, at the Battle for Fort Dusquesne—on the site of present-day Pittsburgh, Pennsylvania—a young Ottawa brave named Pontiac fought on the side of the French forces. A young major by the name of George Washington fought alongside General Braddock, the British commander of the colonial forces. The British had assembled a force of 1,500 against the French and Native American forces of 850. Although the British won the battle, it was only after a loss of 900 men. The Native Americans had been a strong support for the French, and the battle proved to be a training ground for two soldiers who would become famous in the future—Pontiac and Washington.

Young Major George Washington served under General Braddock on the British side in the Battle of Fort Dusquesne.

Lord Jeffrey Amherst led the British forces against Pontiac.

Pontiac's Rebellion

After 1760, the French turned over their forts along the Great Lakes and in the Ohio Valley to the British. This was required by a treaty between the two countries after the British defeated the French in Canada. The Ottawa hoped their new relationship with the British would be as good as the one they had had with the French. But it was not.

The British did not treat Native Americans well. The British seemed to view them as trespassers on the lands they had won from the French. The leader of the British forces at the time, Lord Jeffrey Amherst, considered all Native Americans savages. He changed the trading rules the native people were accustomed to, and this increased bad feelings among the many tribes.

Amherst did not trust any native people. He reduced the number of guns and other supplies that the British could trade with them. Amherst also ended another important custom. The French had always given the natives gifts of blankets and food before beginning the trading. Amherst stopped that policy, which angered the Native Americans. They looked to Pontiac, an Ottawa chief, for help.

Pontiac was a tall, well-built man and a powerful speaker. At meetings around

Pontiac, in an undated engraving.

Pontiac using his charisma and powers of persuasion in council.

council fires, he could skillfully persuade others to change their opinions and adopt his ideas. One of his ideas led to an alliance of Native Americans from many tribes in 1763.

Pontiac believed that a force of Native Americans from many tribes could defeat the British in the Ohio Valley and Great Lakes area. Pontiac was influenced by friends among the French traders and by the message of Native American prophet, Neolin, from the Delaware tribe. Neolin preached that all native people should return to their old ways, regain the use of their lands, and give up their use of European-made goods. The French traders led Pontiac to believe that the French king would send forces to support the Native Americans if they attacked the British.

With these two influences upon him, Pontiac organized an alliance of 1,000 warriors. The group included the Chip-

pewa, Potawatomi, Delaware, Seneca, Shawnee, Winnebago, and Wyandot. This alliance was a major achievement in the history of tribal conflict with whites. Pontiac did what no other Native American had done—unite the members of many tribes, even if for only a short period of time.

Rumors reached Lord Jeffrey Amherst that Pontiac was planning an attack on the British forts in the area. Amherst, who was headquartered in New York, paid no attention to the rumors. He did not believe that a band of uneducated native people could threaten his well-trained and well-fortified forces. The quality of Pontiac's military strategy surprised Amherst.

For nearly a year, the Native American warriors under Pontiac attacked the 14 British forts from Pennsylvania to Lake Superior. In six weeks they captured 10 forts, killing many soldiers and taking hostages. They did not succeed in capturing the three largest forts: Fort Detroit, Fort Pitt, and Fort Niagara.

Pontiac himself, led the siege on Fort Detroit, which began in May 1763. Pontiac's first plan was to get inside the fort by pretending to meet with the commander of the fort about trading matters. Pontiac and his aides went to the meeting with arms concealed under their clothes. They never used them. The commander suspected trouble and had armed soldiers in clear sight of Pontiac at all times.

Failing to launch the attack from inside, Pontiac and his forces surrounding the fort fired on the British. From May until November, the battle raged. Pontiac set up his forces in several lines or layers around the fort. Each line of warriors was distanced from the other. This strategy was intended to prevent supplies and reinforcements from reaching the fort.

The British in the field were astounded that the native warriors could sustain such a long and well-fought battle. Amherst, in New York, was reluctant to send reinforcements, still thinking the native warriors were far inferior to his soldiers. Finally he was convinced of the strength of Pontiac's forces, and over time, enough reinforcements did reach the British to give them the final victory. By November, Pontiac ended the battle. Most of the Native Americans in the alliance were weary of fighting. Many had already left and rejoined their families to begin preparing for the winter hunt.

During Pontiac's rebellion, many British and Native Americans were killed not only at Fort Detroit, but at the other forts. Pontiac finally made peace with the British. In 1765, he signed a treaty never to fight again. He was not able to make peace with all of his own people. Many members of other tribes were angry with Pontiac because the rebellion led to their defeat. In 1769, Pontiac was killed in Cahokia, Illinois, by an unknown Native American.

(Photo courtesy of Bettmann Archive, NY)

Photo of a painting by Frederick Remington showing Pontiac and his men leaving Fort Detroit.

Lost Lands, Changed Ways

The history of the Ottawa from 1789 to 1855 is marked by many treaties with the U.S. government. As a result of these treaties, the tribe lost its original homelands. Year after year, more white settlers invaded Ottawa lands. The settlers illegally cut timber on the tribe's lands and fished in their waterways. And often they simply stole those native people's possessions that they could pick up and carry away.

As more whites invaded the homelands of these Native Americans, their tribal lifestyle began to change. It became difficult to continue the centuries-old traditions of sharing homes and activities in tribal communities. It also became more difficult to live off the land by farming, fishing, and hunting.

The Ottawa came to depend increasingly on the goods they could buy from or trade with whites. And they were building up debts for these goods, debts they could not repay because they had no money. One way for them to pay their debts, according to the whites, was to sell their land.

Piece by piece, the Ottawa lost their lands, but it was not only because they owed money. White settlers, backed by the federal government, put intense pressure on the natives. The whites would eventually gain control of the vast lands the Ottawa had occupied for thousands of years.

In 1795, the Ottawa gave up their rights to lands in Ohio. In 1821, all lands in Michigan south of the Grand River were lost. The Treaty of Chicago in 1833 forced the Ottawa, Chippewa, and Potawatomi of Wisconsin, Illinois, and southern Michigan to move first to Council Bluffs, Iowa, and then to Kansas.

By 1836, efforts were underway to make Michigan a state. But that could not happen unless the Ottawa and Chippewa people in northern Michigan agreed to move off their lands. The Treaty of Washington in 1836 was the result. It was signed by only 21 of the more than 100 Ottawa and Chippewa chiefs, yet the U.S. government expected all Native Americans to honor the treaty. This was contrary to tribal custom, which allowed important changes only if all members of the tribal council agreed.

The Ottawa and Chippewa believed the 1836 treaty allowed them a choice: to remain on their lands north of the Grand

(Photo courtesy of Historical Pictures Service, Chicago)

White men gobbled up Indian land despite meetings and treaties.

River and along the Little Traverse Bay, or to be moved by the U.S. government to lands west of the Mississippi River. But when the treaty was ratified by Congress, the matter of choice was eliminated. The Native Americans were given only five years to remain on their lands, then they had to move.

The 1836 Treaty did have two good features: It paid the Ottawa a yearly allotment of money, and it did not force them to give up their rights to fish in the region.

Most of the Native Americans in the area did not want to be moved West. Some avoided relocation by joining other Ottawa living on Manitoulin Island, across the border in Canada. The island, located where the Michigan and Huron Lakes join, is still home to native people today. Other Ottawa pooled their yearly incomes from the government and bought land in the newly formed state of Michigan. Michigan gained statehood in 1837.

Still others were relocated to the Indian Territory. It was a wilderness west of the Mississippi designated by the U.S.

government in the 1830s as the new homeland for all Eastern tribes. That Indian Territory was to become the state of Oklahoma in 1907, at which time the Native Americans were confined to even smaller plots of land within the area. A few hundred Ottawa still live on these lands in Oklahoma.

The Ottawa people who remained in Michigan wanted to be citizens of the new state. They petitioned the state, and the state petitioned the U.S. government. Finally, in 1850, the Michigan constitution allowed the Ottawa to become citizens, but only if they renounced their tribal membership.

In 1855, the U.S. government signed its last treaty with the Ottawa and Chippewa. The Treaty of Detroit set aside more than 500,000 acres of land along Lake Michigan and Lake Superior for them. Yet, the lands could not be held in common as tribal lands. Instead, the lands had to be owned by individuals. There were so many regulations to ownership that very few Ottawa or Chippewa ever became landowners. Most lands eventually were claimed by whites.

Steele.

The Seneca tribe fought beside the Ottawa against the Europeans. The two Seneca braves pictured here were painted by George Catlin.

String.

The Ottawa Today

During the late-19th and early-20th centuries, the Ottawa and other Native Americans gradually adopted the language and lifestyle of their white neighbors. Education provided by the state and federal government helped to make this happen.

In 1893, a boarding school for Native Americans was established in Mount Pleasant, Michigan. This followed the closing of government day schools. Ottawa parents were displeased to be separated from their children, but most considered the boarding school the best available way to educate their children.

Over the years, hundreds of Native Americans were graduated from Mount Pleasant. In 1933, the school was closed and Native Americans began attending public schools. State support for Native American education was weak until 1972. In that year, the Indian Education Act made it possible for tuition reimbursement for Native Americans attending state colleges or universities in Michigan.

In 1979, the U.S. government set a new policy for dealing with Native Americans. The government would officially recognize a Native American group only if it has a tribal constitution, can prove its ancestors lived in a specific region, and has a continuous line from ancient times to the present. By that definition, the Grand Traverse Band of the Ottawa and Chippewa was among the first to qualify for official recognition by the U.S. government.

This official status is important to any tribe seeking to maintain its legal rights. For example, the U.S. government sued the state of Michigan on behalf of the Ottawa and Chippewa people who were seeking fishing rights based on the Treaty of 1836. The lawsuit regained the rights of those tribes to fish, unrestricted by Michigan laws. But even with the law on their side, these Native Americans are not always able to exercise their fishing rights without interference by those who disagree with the outcome of the lawsuit.

Today, more than 60,000 Native Americans—mostly Ottawa and Chippewa—live in Michigan. This is the largest number of native people in any state east of the Mississippi. Many of the Michigan Native Americans work and live in cities such as Detroit, Grand Rapids, Lansing, Muskegon, Saginaw, and Traverse City.

Several groups, such as the Grand Rapids Inter-Tribal Council, support Native American activities. Council members advise on matters of law, housing, health, education, and culture. As a result, the Ottawa and other tribes in Michigan have preserved their heritage while being active members of their communities.

Important Dates in Ottawa History

1500s	French explorers first make contact with the Ottawa in the Great Lakes region.
1649-1700	The Ottawa control the fur trade with the French.
1755	Pontiac fights on the side of the French against British forces in the battle for Fort Dusquene.
1763	Pontiac's Rebellion unites 1,000 Native Americans of many tribes in their fight against the British forces who hold forts in the Ohio River Valley and along the Great Lakes.
1765	Pontiac makes peace with the British.
1769	Pontiac is killed in Illinois by an unknown Native American.
1795	The Ottawa sign a treaty with the U.S. and give up lands in Ohio.
1821	The Ottawa sign a treaty with the U.S. and give up some lands in Michigan.
1830s	The U.S. government relocates some Ottawa, Chippewa, and Potawatomi to the Indian Territory, land west of the Mississippi River.
1836	By the Treaty of Washington, the Ottawa and Chippewa gave up the last of their tribal lands in Michigan.
1837	Michigan becomes a state.
1850	The state of Michigan grants citizenship to those Ottawa who give up tribal membership.
1855	The Treaty of Detroit is signed. By its terms, Native Americans in Michigan can no longer own lands as a tribe.
1893	A boarding school for Native Americans is established in Mount Pleasant, Michigan.
1933	The Mount Pleasant boarding school closes. It is the last school run by the government for Native Americans in Michigan.
1934	The U.S. government passes the Indian Reorganization Act, allowing reorganization of tribal bands and providing government money for Native American development.
1972	The Indian Education Act provides for college tuition reimbursement for Native Americans attending state colleges and universities in Michigan.
1980	The Grand Traverse Band of the Ottawa and Chippewa people are recognized by the U.S. government as having historical and legal status.
1990s	The Ottawa are among the more than 60,000 Native Americans living and working in Michigan.

INDEX